In Indian Culture

Why do we...

by
Swamini Vimalananda
Radhika Krishnakumar

illustrations
Maniam Selven

Central Chinmaya Mission Trust

© Central Chinmaya Mission Trust

Printed upto	March 2002	- 61000 copies
Reprint	May 2002	- 5000 copies
Reprint	August 2002	- 5000 copies

Published by :
Central Chinmaya Mission Trust
Sandeepany Sadhanalaya
Saki Vihar Road, Mumbai 400 072. India.
Tel.: 857 23 67, 857 58 06 Fax : 091-22-857 3065
Email : chinmaya@bom2.vsnl.net.in

Distribution Centre in USA :
Chinmaya Mission Wesr
Publications Division
560 Bridgetown Pike, Langhorne, PA 19053, USA
Tel.: (215)396-0390 Fax: (215)396-9710
www.chinmayapublications.org
publications@chinmaya.org

Printed by :
Priya Graphics
J-120, Ansa Industrial Estate,
Sakinaka, Mumbai - 400 072. India.
Tel.: 695 99 35 Telefax : 852 80 97

Price : Rs.30.00

FOREWORD

Indian culture is admired and respected all over the world for its beauty and depth. This book features in simple terms, the various aspects of both beauty and depth in this culture. Almost every Indian custom and tradition has either a scientific, logical, historical, social or spiritual significance. Understanding this lends meaning to an otherwise mechanical following of the customs which are often misunderstood to be mere superstitions that fade away in time.

A unique feature of Indian culture is its self-rejuvenating capacity. Customs that are obsolete are gradually dropped as seen in the instances of human sacrifice as well as animal sacrifice to a large extent, sati, untouchability etc. This culture tailors itself constantly to take the best of the modern, technological age without losing its roots.

It is this adaptability that has enabled India to be recognised as one of the world's oldest living civilisations. The customs and traditions selected for these pages are simple, enduring ones, that have lasted the test of time and are an integral part of many an Indian home even today.

Pujya Gurudev Swami Chinmayanandaji laid great emphasis on explaining the symbolism in Hindu dharma in a manner that was logical, scientific and appealing to modern man, thereby creating a magnificent cultural renaissance.

This book is dedicated to this great master who spent his entire life in raising the dignity of Indian culture and philosophy in the eyes of the world.

CONTENTS

Why do we light a lamp?.. 1

Why do we have a prayer room?........................... 5

Why do we do *namaste*?....................................... 9

Why do we prostrate
before parents and elders?.................................... 12

Why do we wear marks
on the forehead?... 16

Why do we not touch papers,
books and people with the feet?......................... 20

Why do we apply the holy ash?.......................... 24

Why do we offer food to the Lord
before eating it?... 28

Why do we do *pradakshina*?................................ 33

Why do we regard trees
and plants as sacred?... 37

Why do we fast?... 40

Why do we ring the bell in a temple? 44

Why do we worship the *kalashа*? 47

Why do we worship *tulasi*? 51

Why do we consider the lotus
as special? 55

Why do we blow the conch? 59

Why do we say *shaanti* thrice? 63

Why do we offer a coconut? 67

Why do we chant *Om*? 71

Why do we do *aarati*? 75

Why do we light a lamp?

In almost every Indian home a lamp is lit daily before the altar of the Lord. In some houses it is lit at dawn, in some, twice a day – at dawn and dusk – and in a few it is maintained continuously (*akhanda deepa*). All auspicious functions and moments like daily worship, rituals and festivals and even many social occasions like inaugurations commence with the lighting of the lamp, which is often maintained right through the occasion.

❖   Why do we light a lamp?

Light symbolizes knowledge, and darkness, ignorance. The Lord is the "Knowledge Principle" (*chaitanya*) who is the source, the enlivener and the illuminator of all knowledge. Hence light is worshipped as the Lord Himself.

Knowledge removes ignorance just as light removes darkness. Also knowledge is a lasting inner

wealth by which all outer achievement can be accomplished. Hence we light the lamp to bow down to knowledge as the greatest of all forms of wealth. Knowledge backs all our actions whether good or bad. We therefore keep a lamp lit during all auspicious occasions as a witness to our thoughts and actions.

Why not light a bulb or tube light? That too would remove darkness. But the traditional oil lamp has a further spiritual significance. The oil or ghee in the lamp symbolizes our *vaasanas* or negative tendencies and the wick, the ego. When lit by spiritual knowledge, the *vaasanas* get slowly exhausted and the ego too finally perishes. The flame of a lamp always burns upwards. Similarly we should acquire such knowledge as to take us towards higher ideals.

A single lamp can light hundreds more just as a man of knowledge can give it to many more. The brilliance of the light does not diminish despite its repeated use to light many more lamps. So too knowledge does not lessen when shared with or imparted to others. On the contrary it increases in clarity and conviction on giving. It benefits both the receiver and the giver.

Whilst lighting the lamp we thus pray:

दीपज्योतिः परब्रह्म दीप: सर्वतमोऽपह:
दीपेन साध्यते सर्वं सन्ध्यादीपो नमोऽस्तु ते।।

Deepajyotihi parabrahma
   Deepa sarva tamopahaha
Deepena saadhyate sarvam
   Sandhyaa deepo namostute

*I prostrate to the dawn/dusk lamp, whose light
is the Knowledge Principle (the Supreme Lord),
which removes the darkness of ignorance and
by which all can be achieved in life.*

Which else shall beautify a home
      But the flame of a lovely lamp?
Which else shall adorn the mind
      But the light of wisdom deep?

                    – Swami Chinmayananda .

Thus this custom contains a wealth of intellectual
and spiritual meaning.

Why do we have a prayer room?

Most Indian homes have a prayer room or altar. A lamp is lit and the Lord worshipped each day. Other spiritual practices like *japa* (repetition of the Lord's name), meditation, *paaraayana* (reading of the scriptures), prayers, devotional singing etc. is also done here. Special worship is done on auspicious occasions like birthdays, anniversaries, festivals and the like. Each member of the family – young or old – communes with and worships the Divine here.

❖ Why do we have a prayer room?

The Lord is the owner of the entire creation. He is therefore the true owner of the house we live in too. The prayer room is the Master room of the house. We are the earthly occupants of His property. This notion rids us of false pride and possessiveness.

5

The ideal attitude to take is to regard the Lord as the true owner of our homes and ourselves as caretakers of His home. But if that is rather difficult, we could at least think of Him as a very welcome guest. Just as we would house an important guest in the best comfort, so too we felicitate the Lord's presence in our homes by having a prayer room or altar, which is, at all times, kept clean and well-decorated.

Also the Lord is all-pervading. To remind us that He resides in our homes with us, we have prayer rooms. Without the grace of the Lord, no task can be successfully or easily accomplished. We invoke His grace by communing with Him in the prayer room each day and on special occasions.

Each room in a house is dedicated to a specific function like the bedroom for resting, the drawing room to receive guests, the kitchen for cooking etc. The furniture, decor and the atmosphere of each room are made conducive to the purpose it serves. So too for the purpose of meditation, worship and prayer, we should have a conducive atmosphere – hence the need for a prayer room.

Sacred thoughts and sound vibrations pervade the place and influence the minds of those who spend time there. Spiritual thoughts and vibrations accumulated through regular meditation, worship and chanting done there pervade the prayer room. Even when we are tired or agitated, by just sitting in the prayer room for a while, we feel calm, rejuvenated and spiritually uplifted.

Why do we do *namaste?*

Indians greet each other with *namaste*. The two palms are placed together in front of the chest and the head bows whilst saying the word *namaste*. This greeting is for all – people younger than us, of our own age, those older than us, friends and even strangers.

There are five forms of formal traditional greeting enjoined in the *shaastras* of which *namaskaaram* is one. This is understood as prostration but it actually refers to paying homage as we do today when we greet each other with a *namaste*.

❖ Why do we do *namaste?*

Namaste could be just a casual or formal greeting, a cultural convention or an act of worship. However there is much more to it than meets the eye. In Sanskrit *namah* + *te* = *namaste*. It means – I bow to you – my greetings, salutations or prostration to you.

Namaha can also be literally interpreted as *"na ma"* (not mine). It has a spiritual significance of negating or reducing one's ego in the presence of another.

The real meeting between people is the meeting of their minds. When we greet another, we do so with *namaste,* which means, "may our minds meet," indicated by the folded palms placed before the chest. The bowing down of the head is a gracious form of extending friendship in love and humility.

The spiritual meaning is even deeper. The life force, the divinity, the Self or the Lord in me is the same in all. Recognising this oneness with the meeting of the palms, we salute with head bowed the Divinity in the person we meet. That is why sometimes, we close our eyes as we do *namaste* to a revered person or the Lord – as if to look within. The gesture is often accompanied by words like "Ram Ram", "Jai Shri Krishna", "Namo Narayana", "Jai Siya Ram", "Om Shanti" etc – indicating the recognition of this divinity.

When we know this significance, our greeting does not remain just a superficial gesture or word but paves the way for a deeper communion with another in an atmosphere of love and respect.

Why do we prostrate before parents and elders?

Indians prostrate to their parents, elders, teachers and noble souls by touching their feet. The elder in turn blesses us by placing his or her hand on or over our heads. Prostration is done daily, when we meet elders and particularly on important occasions like the beginning of a new task, birthdays, festivals etc. In certain traditional circles, prostration is accompanied by *abhivaadana* which serves to introduce oneself, announce one's family and social stature.

❖ Why do we offer prostrations?

Man stands on his feet. Touching the feet in prostration is a sign of respect for the age, maturity, nobility and divinity that our elders personify. It symbolizes our recognition of their selfless love for us and the sacrifices that they have done for our welfare. It is a way of humbly acknowledging the

greatness of another. This tradition reflects the strong family ties which has been one of India's enduring strengths.

The good wishes (*sankalpa*) and blessings (*aashirvaada*) of elders are highly valued in India. We prostrate to seek them. Good thoughts create positive vibrations. Good wishes springing from a heart full of love, divinity and nobility have a tremendous strength. When we prostrate with humility and respect, we invoke the good wishes and blessings of elders which flow in the form of positive energy to envelop us. This is why the posture assumed whether it is in the standing or prone position, enables the entire body to receive the energy thus received.

The different forms of showing respect are:

◇ *Pratuthana* – rising to welcome a person.

◇ *Namaskaara* – paying homage in the form of *namaste* (discussed separately in this book).

◇ *Upasangrahan* – touching the feet of elders or teachers.

◇ *Shaashtaanga* – prostrating fully with the feet, knees, stomach, chest, forehead and arms touching the ground in front of the elder.

✧ *Pratyabivaadana* – returning a greeting.

Rules are prescribed in our scriptures as to who should prostrate to whom. Wealth, family name, age, moral strength and spiritual knowledge in ascending order of importance qualified men to receive respect. This is why a king though the ruler of the land, would prostrate before a spiritual master. Epics like the *Ramayana* and *Mahabharata* have many stories highlighting this aspect.

This tradition thus creates an environment of mutual love and respect among people ensuring harmony in the family and society.

Why do we wear marks on the forehead?

Most religious Indians, especially married women wear a *tilak* or *pottu* on the forehead. It is applied daily after a bath and on special occasions, before or after ritualistic worship or a visit to the temple. In many communities, it is enjoined upon married women to sport a *kumkum* mark on their foreheads at all times. The orthodox put it on with due rituals. The *tilak* is applied on saints and images of the Lord as a form of worship and in many parts of North India as a respectful form of welcome, to honour guests or when bidding farewell to a son or husband about to embark on a journey. The *tilak* varies in colour and form.

This custom was not prevalent in the *vedic* period. It gained popularity in the *pauranic* period. Some believe that it originated in South India.

❖ Why do we wear marks (*tilak*, *pottu* and the like) on the forehead?

The *tilak* or *pottu* invokes a feeling of sanctity in the wearer and others. It is recognised as a religious mark. Its form and colour vary according to one's caste, religious sect or the form of the Lord worshipped.

In earlier times, the four castes (based on *varna* or colour) – *Braahmana*, *Kshatriya*, *Vaishya* and *Sudra* – applied marks differently. The *brahmin* applied a white *chandan* mark signifying purity as his profession was of a priestly or academic nature. The *kshatriya* applied a red *kumkum* mark signifying valour as he belonged to the warrior races. The *vaishya* wore a yellow *kesar* or turmeric mark signifying prosperity as he was a businessman or trader devoted to creation of wealth. The *sudra* applied a black *bhasma*, *kasturi* or charcoal mark signifying service as he supported the work of the other three divisions. Also Vishnu worshippers apply a *chandan tilak* of the shape of "U", Shiva worshippers a *tripundra* (of the shape of "≡") of *bhasma*, Devi worshippers a red dot of *kumkum* and so on.

The *chandan, kumkum* or *bhasma* which is offered to the Lord is taken back as *prasad* and applied on our foreheads. The *tilak* covers the spot between the eyebrows, which is the seat of memory and thinking. It is known as the *Aajna Chakra* in the language of Yoga. The *tilak* is applied with the prayer – "May I remember the Lord. May this pious feeling pervade all my activities. May I be righteous in my deeds." Even when we temporarily forget this prayerful attitude the mark on another reminds us of our resolve. The *tilak* is thus a blessing of the Lord and a protection against wrong tendencies and forces.

The entire body emanates energy in the form of electromagnetic waves – the forehead and the subtle spot between the eyebrows especially so. That is why worry generates heat and causes a headache. The *tilak* or *pottu* cools the forehead, protects us and prevents energy loss. Sometimes the entire forehead is covered with *chandan* or *bhasma*. Using plastic reusable "stick bindis" is not very beneficial, even though it serves the purpose of decoration.

This custom is unique to Indians and helps to easily identify us anywhere.

Why do we not touch papers, books and people with the feet?

In Indian homes, we are taught from a very young age, never to touch papers, books and people with our feet. If the feet accidentally touch papers, books, musical instruments or any other educational equipment, children are told to reverentially touch what was stamped with their hands and then touch their eyes as a mark of apology.

❖ Why do we not touch papers and people with the feet?

To Indians, knowledge is sacred and divine. So it must be given respect at all times. Nowadays we separate subjects as sacred and secular. But in ancient India every subject – academic or spiritual – was considered divine and taught by the guru in the *gurukula*.

The custom of not stepping on educational tools is a frequent reminder of the high position accorded to knowledge in Indian culture. From an early age, this wisdom fosters in us a deep reverence for books and education. This is also the reason why we worship books, vehicles and instruments once a year on *Saraswathi Pooja* or *Ayudha Pooja* day, dedicated to the Goddess of Learning. In fact, each day before starting our studies, we pray:

सरस्वति नमस्तुभ्यं वरदे कामरूपिणी
विद्यारंभं करिष्यामि सिद्धिर्भवतु मे सदा।।

Saraswati namasthubhyam
Varade kaama roopini
Vidyaarambham karishyaami
Sidhirbhavatu mé sadaa

O Goddess Saraswati, the giver of
boons and fulfiller of wishes,
I prostrate to You before
starting my studies.
May You always fulfill me.

Children are also strongly discouraged from touching people with their feet. Even if this happens accidentally, we touch the person and bring the fingers to our eyes as a mark of apology. Even when elders touch a younger person inadvertently with their feet, they immediately apologize.

❖ To touch another with the feet is considered an act of misdemeanor. Why is this so?

Man is regarded as the most beautiful, living, breathing temple of the Lord! Therefore touching another with the feet is akin to disrespecting the divinity within him or her. This calls for an immediate apology, which is offered with reverence and humility.

Thus, many of our customs are designed to be simple but powerful reminders or pointers of profound philosophical truths. This is one of the factors that has kept Indian culture alive across centuries.

Why do we apply the holy ash?

The ash of any burnt object is not regarded as holy ash. *Bhasma* (the holy ash) is the ash from the *homa* (sacrificial fire) where special wood along with ghee and other herbs is offered as worship of the Lord. Or the deity is worshipped by pouring ash as *abhisheka* and is then distributed as *bhasma*.

Bhasma is generally applied on the forehead. Some apply it on certain parts of the body like the upper arms, chest etc. Some ascetics rub it all over the body. Many consume a pinch of it each time they receive it.

❖ Why do we do use *bhasma?*

The word *bhasma* means "that by which our sins are destroyed and the Lord is remembered". *Bha* implies *bhartsanam* ("to destroy") and *sma* implies *smaranam* ("to remember"). The application of *bhasma* therefore signifies destruction of the evil and

remembrance of the divine. *Bhasma* is called *vibhuti* (which means "glory") as it gives glory to one who applies it and *raksha* (which means a source of protection) as it protects the wearer from ill health and evil, by purifying him or her.

Homa (offering of oblations into the fire with sacred chants) signifies the offering or surrender of the ego and egocentric desires into the flame of knowledge or a noble and selfless cause. The consequent ash signifies the purity of the mind which results from such actions. Also the fire of knowledge burns the oblation and wood signifying ignorance and inertia respectively. The ash we apply indicates that we should burn false identification with the body and become free of the limitations of birth and death. The application of ash also reminds us that the body is perishable and shall one day be reduced to ashes. We should therefore not get too attached to it. Death can come at any moment and this awareness must increase our drive to make the best use of time. This is not to be misconstrued as a morose reminder of death but as a powerful pointer towards the fact that time and tide wait for none.

Bhasma is specially associated with Lord Shiva who applies it all over His body. Shiva devotees apply *bhasma* as a *tripundra* (the form of "≡"). When applied with a red spot in the centre, the mark symbolises Shiva-Shakti (the unity of energy and matter that creates the entire seen and unseen universe).

Ash is what remains when all the wood is burnt away and it does not decay. Similarly, the Lord is the imperishable Truth that remains when the entire creation of innumerable names and forms is dissolved.

Bhasma has medicinal value and is used in many ayurvedic medicines. It absorbs excess moisture from the body and prevents colds and headaches. The *Upanishads* say that the famous *Mrityunjaya mantra* should be chanted whilst applying ash on the forehead.

त्र्यंबकं यजामहे सुगन्धिं पुष्टिवर्धनम् ।
उर्वारुकमिव बन्धनान् मृत्योर्मुक्षीय मा अमृतात् ।।

Tryambakam yajaamahe
Sugandhim pushtivardhanam
Urvaa rukamiva bhandhanaan
Mrytyor muksheeyamaa amrutaat

"We worship the three-eyed Lord Shiva who nourishes and spreads fragrance in our lives. May He free us from the shackles of sorrow, change and death - effortlessly, like the fall of a ripe brinjal from its stem."

Why do we offer food to the Lord before eating it?

In western tradition food is partaken after a thanksgiving prayer – grace. Indians make an offering of it to the Lord and later partake of it as *prasaada* – a holy gift from the Lord. In temples and in many homes, the cooked food is first offered to the Lord each day. The offered food is mixed with the rest of the food and then served as *prasaada*. In our daily ritualistic worship (*pooja*) too we offer *naivedyam* (food) to the Lord. Why do we do so?

❖ Why do we offer *neivedya*?

The Lord is omnipotent and omniscient. Man is a part, while the Lord is the totality. All that we do is by His strength and knowledge alone. Hence what we receive in life as a result of our actions is really His alone. We acknowledge this through the act of offering food to Him. This is exemplified by the Hindu

words *tera tujko arpan* from the arati "Jai Jagadisha Hare" – I offer what is Yours to You. Thereafter it is akin to His gift to us, graced by His divine touch.

Knowing this, our entire attitude to food and the act of eating changes. The food offered will naturally be pure and the best. We share what we get with others before consuming it. We do not demand, complain or criticise the quality of the food we get. We do not waste or reject it. We eat it with cheerful acceptance (*prasaada buddhi*). When we become established in this attitude, it goes beyond the perview of food and pervades our entire lives. We are then able to cheerfully accept all we get in life as His *prasaada*.

Before we partake of our daily meals we first sprinkle water around the plate as an act of purification. Five morsels of food are placed on the side of the plate acknowledging the debt owed by us to the

- divine forces (*devta runa*) for their benign grace and protection;
- our ancestors (*pitru runa*) for giving us their lineage and a family culture;

- the sages (*rishi runa*) as our religion and culture have been "realised", maintained and handed down to us by them;

- our fellow beings (*manushya runa*) who constitute society without the support of which we could not live as we do and

- other living beings (*bhuta runa*) for serving us selflessly.

Thereafter the Lord, the life force, who is also within us as the five life-giving physiological functions, is offered the food. This is done with the chant – *praanaaya swaahaa, apaanaaya swaahaa, vyaanaaya swaahaa, udaanaaya swaahaa, samaanaaya swahaa, brahmane swaahaa* (referring to the five physiological functions – respiratory (*praana*), excretory (*apaana*), circulatory (*vyaana*), digestive (*samaana*) and reversal (*udaana*) systems. After offering the food thus, it is eaten as *prasaada* – blessed food.

To remember this concept, many chant the following verses of the *Geeta*.

ब्रह्मार्पणं ब्रह्महविः ब्रह्माग्नौ ब्रह्मणाहुतम्।

ब्रह्मैव तेन गन्तव्यं ब्रह्मकर्मसमाधिना।।

Brahmaarpanam Brahmahavihi
    Brahmaagnau Brahmanaahutam
Brahmaivatenagantavyam
    Brahmakarma samaadhina

    Brahman is the oblation; the clarified butter; the oblation; the fire... Brahman (the Supreme) shall be reached by him who sees the Supreme in all actions.

अहं वैश्वानरो भूत्वा प्राणिनां देहमाश्रितः।

प्राणापान समायुक्तः पचाम्यन्नं चतुर्विधम्।।

Aham vaishvaanarobhutvaa
    praaninaam dehamaashritaha
Praanaapaanasamaayuktaha
    pachaamyannam chaturvidham

    "Residing in all living beings as the digestive fire, I digest the four types of food eaten by them (as an offering to Me)".

Why do we do *pradakshina*?

When we visit a temple, after offering prayers, we circumambulate the *sanctum sanctorum*. This is called *pradakshina*.

❖ Why do we do *pradakshina*?

We cannot draw a circle without a centre point. The Lord is the centre, source and essence of our lives. Recognising Him as the focal point in our lives, we go about doing our daily chores. This is the significance of *pradakshina*.

Also every point on the circumference of a circle is equidistant from the centre. This means that wherever or whoever we may be, we are equally close to the Lord. His grace flows towards us without partiality.

❖ Why is *pradakshina* done only in a clockwise manner?

The reason is not, as a person said, to avoid a traffic jam! As we do *pradakshina*, the Lord is always on our right. In India the right side symbolises auspiciousness. It is a telling fact that even in the English language it is called the "right" side and not the wrong one! So as we circumambulate the *sanctum sanctorum* we remind ourselves to lead an auspicious life of righteousness, with the Lord who is the indispensable source of help and strength, as our guide – the "right hand" – the *dharma* aspect – of our lives. We thereby overcome our wrong tendencies and avoid repeating the sins of the past.

Indian scriptures enjoin – *matrudevo bhava, pitrudevo bhava, acharyadevo bhava.* May you consider your parents and teachers as you would the Lord. With this in mind we also do *pradakshina* around our parents and divine personages. The story of Lord Ganesha circumambulating his parents is a well-known one.

After the completion of traditional worship (*pooja*), we customarily do *pradakshina* around ourselves. In this way we recognise and remember the supreme divinity within us, which alone is idolised in the form of the Lord that we worship outside.

As we circumambulate, we chant:

यानि कानि च पापानि जन्मान्तरकृतानि च
तानि तानि विनश्यन्ति प्रदक्षिण पदे पदे।।

Yaani kaani cha paapaani
   janmaantara krtaani cha
taani taani vinashyanti
   pradakshina pade pade.

"All the sins committed by an individual from innumerable past births are destroyed by each step taken whilst doing pradakshina.*"*

Why do we regard trees and plants as sacred?

From ancient times, Indians have worshipped plants and trees and regarded all flora and fauna as sacred. This is not an old fashioned or uncivilised practice. It reveals the sensitivity, foresight and refinement of Indian culture. While modern man often works to "conquer" Mother Nature, ancient Indians "worshipped" her.

❖ Why do we regard plants and trees as sacred?

The Lord, the life in us, pervades all living beings, be they plants or animals. Hence, they are all regarded as sacred. Human life on earth depends on plants and trees. They give us the vital factors that makes life possible on earth: food, oxygen, clothing, shelter, medicines etc. They lend beauty to our surroundings. They serve man without expectation and sacrifice themselves to sustain us. They epitomise sacrifice. If a stone is thrown on a fruit-laden tree, the tree in turn gives fruit!

In fact, the flora and fauna owned the earth before man appeared on it. Presently, the world is seriously threatened by the destruction of forestlands and the extinction of many species of vegetation due to man's callous attitude toward them. We protect only what we value. Hence, in India, we are taught to regard trees and plants as sacred. Naturally, we will then protect them.

Indian scriptures tell us to plant ten trees if, for any reason, we have to cut one. We are advised to use parts of trees and plants only as much as is needed for food, fuel, shelter etc. We are also urged to apologise to a plant or tree before cutting it to avoid incurring a specific sin named s*oona*. In our childhood, we are told stories of the sacrifice and service done by plants and trees and about our duty to plant and nourish them. Certain trees and plants like *tulasi, peepal* etc., which have tremendous beneficial qualities, are worshipped till today.

It is believed that divine beings manifest as trees and plants, and many people worship them to fulfill their desires or to please the Lord.

Why do we fast?

Most devout Indians fast regularly or on special occasions like festivals. On such days they do not eat at all, eat once or make do with fruits or a special diet of simple food. Some undertake rigorous fasts when they do not even drink water the whole day! Fasting is done for many reasons – to please the Lord, to discipline oneself and even to protest. Gandhiji fasted to protest against the British rule.

❖ Why do we fast?

Is it to save food or to create an appetite to feast after the fast? Not really. Then why do we fast?

Fasting in Sanskrit is called *upavaasa*. *Upa* means "near" + v*aasa* means "to stay". *Upavaasa* therefore means staying near (the Lord), meaning the attainment of close mental proximity with the Lord. Then what has *upavaasa* to do with food?

A lot of our time and energy is spent in procuring food items, preparing, cooking, eating and digesting food. Certain food types make our minds dull and agitated. Hence on certain days man decides to save time and conserve his energy by eating either simple, light food or totally abstaining from eating so that his mind becomes alert and pure. The mind, otherwise pre-occupied by the thought of food, now entertains noble thoughts and stays with the Lord. Since it is a self-imposed form of discipline it is usually adhered to with joy.

Also every system needs a break and an overhaul to work at its best. Rest and a change of diet during fasting is very good for the digestive system and the entire body.

The more you indulge the senses, the more they make their demands. Fasting helps us to cultivate control over our senses, sublimate our desires and guide our minds to be poised and at peace.

Fasting should not make us weak, irritable or create an urge to indulge later. This happens when there is no noble goal behind fasting. Some fast, rather they diet, merely to reduce weight. Others fast as a vow to please the Lord or to fulfill their desires, some to develop will power, control the senses, some as a form of austerity and so on. The *Bhagavad Geeta* urges us to eat appropriately – neither too less nor too much – *yukta-aahaara* and to eat simple, pure and healthy food (a *saatvik* diet) even when not fasting.

Why do we ring the bell in a temple?

In most temples there are one or more bells hung from the top, near the entrance. The devotee rings the bell as soon as he enters, thereafter proceeding for *darshan* of the Lord and prayers. Children love jumping up or being carried high in order to reach the bell.

❖ Why do we ring the bell?

Is it to wake up the Lord? But the Lord never sleeps. Is it to let the Lord know we have come? He does not need to be told, as He is all-knowing. Is it a form of seeking permission to enter His precinct? It is a homecoming and therefore entry needs no permission. The Lord welcomes us at all times. Then why do we ring the bell?

The ringing of the bell produces what is regarded as an auspicious sound. It produces the sound *Om,* the universal name of the Lord. There should be auspiciousness within and without, to gain the vision of the Lord who is all-auspiciousness.

Even while doing the ritualistic *aarati*, we ring the bell. It is sometimes accompanied by the auspicious sounds of the conch and other musical instruments. An added significance of ringing the bell, conch and other instruments is that they help drowned any inauspicious or irrelevant noises and comments that might disturb or distract the worshippers in their devotional ardour, concentration and inner peace.

As we start the daily ritualistic worship (*pooja*) we ring the bell, chanting:

आगमार्थं तु देवानां गमनार्थं तु रक्षसाम्
कुर्वे घण्टारवं तत्र देवताह्वान लक्षणम्।।

Aagamaarthamtu devaanaam
 gamanaarthamtu rakshasaam
Kurve ghantaaravam tatra
 devataahvaahna lakshanam

I ring this bell indicating
 the invocation of divinity,
So that virtuous and noble forces
 enter (my home and heart);
And the demonic and evil forces
From within and without, depart.

Why do we worship the *kalasha?*

First of all what is a *kalasha?* A brass, mud or copper pot is filled with water. Mango leaves are placed in the mouth of the pot and a coconut is placed over it. A red or white thread is tied around its neck or sometimes all around it in an intricate diamond-shaped pattern. The pot may be decorated with designs. Such a pot is known as a *kalasha.* When the pot is filled with water or rice, it is known as *purnakumbha* representing the inert body which when filled with the divine life force gains the power to do all the wonderful things that makes life what it is.

A *kalasha* is placed with due rituals on all important occasions like the traditional house warming (*grhapravesa*), wedding, daily worship etc. It is placed near the entrance as a sign of welcome. It is also used in a traditional manner while receiving holy personages.

❖ Why do we worship the *kalasha?*

Before the creation came into being, Lord Vishnu was reclining on His snake-bed in the milky ocean. From His navel emerged a lotus from which appeared Lord Brahma, the Creator, who thereafter created this world. The water in the *kalasha* symbolises the primordial water from which the entire creation emerged. It is the giver of life to all and has the potential of creating innumerable names and forms, the inert objects and the sentient beings and all that is auspicious. in the world from the energy behind the universe. The leaves and coconut represent creation. The thread represents the love that "binds" all in creation. The *kalasha* is therefore considered auspicious and worshipped.

The waters from all the holy rivers, the knowledge of all the *Vedas* and the blessings of all the deities are invoked in the *kalasha* and its water is thereafter used for all the rituals, including the *abhisheka*. The consecration (*kumbhaabhisheka*) of a temple is done in a grand manner with elaborate rituals including the pouring of one or more *kalashas* of holy water on the top of the temple.

When the *asuras* and the *devas* churned the milky ocean, the Lord appeared bearing the pot of nectar, which blessed one with everlasting life. Thus the *kalasha* also symbolises immortality.

Men of wisdom are full and complete as they identify with the infinite Truth (*poornatvam*). They brim with joy and love and represent all that is auspicious. We greet them with a *purnakumbha* ("full pot") acknowledging their greatness and as a sign of respectful and reverential welcome, with a "full heart".

Why do we worship *tulasi*?

Either in the front, back or central courtyard of most Indian homes there is a *tulasi-matham* – an altar bearing a *tulasi* plant. In the present day apartments too, many maintain a potted *tulasi* plant. The lady of the house lights a lamp, waters the plant, worships and circumambulates it. The stem, leaves, seeds and even the soil, which provides it a base, are considered holy. A *tulasi* leaf is always placed in the food offered to the Lord. It is also offered to the Lord during *poojas*, especially to Lord Vishnu and His incarnations.

❖ Why do we worship the *tulasi*?

In Sanskrit, *tulanaa naasti athaiva tulasi* – that which is incomparable (in its qualities) is the *tulasi*. For Indians it is one of the most sacred plants. In fact it is known to be the only thing used in worship

51

which, once used, can be washed and reused in *pooja* - as it is regarded so self-purifying.

As one story goes, Tulasi was the devoted wife of Shankhachuda, a celestial being. She believed that Lord Krishna tricked her into sinning. So she cursed Him to become a stone (*shaaligraama*). Seeing her devotion and adherence to righteousness, the Lord blessed her saying that she would become the worshipped plant, *tulasi* that would adorn His head. Also that all offerings would be incomplete without the *tulasi* leaf – hence the worship of *tulasi*.

She also symbolises Goddess Lakshmi, the consort of Lord Vishnu. Those who wish to be righteous and have a happy family life worship the *tulasi*. Tulasi is married to the Lord with all pomp and show as in any wedding. This is because according to another legend, the Lord blessed her to be His consort.

Satyabhama once weighed Lord Krishna against all her legendary wealth. The scales did not balance till a single *tulasi* leaf was placed along with the wealth on the scale by Rukmini with devotion. Thus the *tulasi* played the vital role of demonstrating to the world that even a small object offerred with devotion means more to the Lord than all the wealth in the world.

The *tulasi* leaf has great medicinal value and is used to cure various ailments, including the common cold.

यन्मूले सर्व तीर्थानि यन्नग्रे सर्व देवता
यन्मध्ये सर्व वेदाश्च तुलसी तां नमाम्यहम्।।

Yanmule sarvatirthaani
yannagre sarvadevataa
Yanmadhye sarvavedaascha
tulasi taam namaamyaham

I bow down to the tulasi,
at whose base are all the holy places,
at whose top reside all the deities and
in whose middle are all the Vedas.

Why do we consider the lotus as special?

The lotus is India's national flower and rightly so. Not long ago, the lakes and ponds of India were full of many hued lotuses.

❖ Why do we consider the lotus special?

The lotus is the symbol of truth, auspiciousness and beauty (*satyam, shivam, sundaram*). The Lord is also that nature and therefore, His various aspects are compared to a lotus (i.e. lotus-eyes, lotus feet, lotus hands, the lotus of the heart etc.). Our scriptures and ancient literature extol the beauty of the lotus. Art and architecture also portray the lotus in various decorative motifs and paintings. Many people have names of or related to the lotus: Padma, Pankaja, Kamal, Kamala, Kamalakshi etc. The Goddess of wealth, Lakshmi, sits on a lotus and carries one in Her hand.

The lotus blooms with the rising sun and closes at night. Similarly, our minds open up and expand with the light of knowledge. The lotus grows even in slushy areas. It remains beautiful and untainted despite its surroundings, reminding us that we too can and should strive to remain pure and beautiful within, under all circumstances. The lotus leaf never gets wet even though it is always in water. It symbolises the man of wisdom (*gnaani*) who remains ever joyous, unaffected by the world of sorrow and change. This is revealed in a *shloka* from the *Bhagavad Geeta*:

ब्रह्मण्याधाय कर्माणि सङ्गं त्यक्त्वा करोति यः
लिप्यते न स पापेन पद्मपत्रमिवाम्भसा।।

Brahmanyaadhaaya karmaani
  sangam tyaktvaa karoti yaha
Lipyate na sa paapena
  padma patram ivaambhasaa

He who does actions, offering them to Brahman (the Supreme), abandoning attachment, is not tainted by sin, just as a lotus leaf remains unaffected by the water on it.

From this, we learn that what is natural to the man of wisdom becomes a discipline to be practised by *all saadhakas* or spiritual seekers and devotees.

Our bodies have certain energy centres described in the *Yoga Shaastras* as *chakras*. Each one is associated with lotus that have a certain number of petals. For example, the *Sahasra chakra* at the top of the head, which opens when the *yogi* attains Godhood or Realisation, is represented by a lotus with a thousand petals. Also, the lotus posture (*padmaasana*) is recommended when one sits for meditation.

A lotus emerged from the navel of Lord Vishnu. Lord Brahma originated from it to create the world. Hence, the lotus symbolises the link between the creator and the supreme Cause. It also symbolises *Brahmaloka*, the abode of Lord Brahma.

The auspicious sign of the *swastika* is said to have evolved from the lotus.

From the above, we can well appreciate why the lotus is India's national flower and so special to Indians.

Why do we blow the conch?

In temples or at homes, the conch is blown once or several times before ritualistic worship *(pooja)*. It is sometimes blown whilst doing *aarati* or to mark an auspicious occasion. It is blown before a battle starts or to announce the victory of an army. It is also placed in the altar and worshipped.

When the conch is blown, the primordial sound of *Om* emanates. *Om* is an auspicious sound that was chanted by the Lord before creating the world. It represents the world and the Truth behind it.

As the story goes, the demon Shankhaasura defeated the *devas*, stole the *Vedas* and went to the bottom of the ocean. The *devas* appealed to Lord Vishnu for help. He incarnated as *Matsya Avataara* – the "fish incarnation" and killed Shankhaasura. The Lord blew the conch-shaped bone of his ear and head. The *Om* sound emanated, from which emerged

the *Vedas*. All knowledge enshrined in the *Vedas* is an elaboration of *Om*. The conch therefore is known as *shankha* after Shankhaasura. The conch blown by the Lord is called *Paanchajanya*. He carries it at all times in one of His four hands. It represents *dharma* or righteousness that is one of the four goals (*purushaarthas*) of life. The sound of the conch is thus also the victory call of good over evil. If we place a conch close to our ears, we hear the sound of the waves of the ocean.

Another well-known purpose of blowing the conch and other instruments, known traditionally to produce auspicious sounds is to drown or mask negative comments or noises that may disturb or upset the atmosphere or the minds of worshippers.

Ancient India lived in her villages. Each village was presided over by a primary temple and several smaller ones. During the *aarati* performed after all important *poojas* and on sacred occasions, the conch used to be blown. Since villages were generally small, the sound of the conch would be heard all over the village. People who could not make it to the temple were reminded to stop whatever they were doing, at least for a few seconds, and mentally bow to the

Lord. The conch sound served to briefly elevate people's minds to a prayerful attitude even in the middle of their busy daily routine.

The conch is placed at the altar in temples and homes next to the Lord as a symbol of *Naada Brahma* (Truth), the V*edas, Om, dharma*, victory and auspiciousness. It is often used to offer devotees *thirtha* (sanctified water) to raise their minds to the highest Truth.

It is worshipped with the following verse.

त्वं पुरा सागरोत्पन्नः विष्णुना विधृतः करे।
देवैश्च पूजितः सर्वैः पाञ्चजन्य नमोऽस्तु ते।।

Twam puraa saagarot pannaha
Vishnunaa vidhrutahakare
Devaischa poojitha sarvaihi
Paanchajanya namostu te

Salutations to Paanchajanya,
the conch born of the ocean,
Held in the hand of Lord Vishnu
and worshipped by all the devaas.

Why do we say *shaanti* thrice?

Shaanti, meaning "peace", is a natural state of being. Disturbances are created either by us or others. For example, peace already exists in a place until someone makes noise. Therefore, peace underlies all our agitations. When agitations end, peace is naturally experienced since it was already there. Where there is peace, there is happiness. Therefore, every one without exception desires peace in his/her life. However, peace within or without seems very hard to attain because it is covered by our ownagitations. A rare few manage to remain peaceful within even in the midst of external agitation and troubles. To invoke peace, we chant prayers. By chanting prayers, troubles end and peace is experienced internally, irrespective of the external disturbances. All such prayers end by chanting *shaanti* thrice.

❖ Why do we say *shaanti* thrice ?

It is believed that *trivaram satyam* – that which is said thrice comes true. For emphasising a point we repeat a thing thrice. In the court of law also, one who takes the witness stand says, "I shall speak the truth, the whole truth and nothing but the truth". We chant *shaanti* thrice to emphasise our intense desire for peace.

All obstacles, problems and sorrows originate from three sources.

1. *Aadhidaivika*: The unseen divine forces over which we have little or no control like earthquakes, floods, volcanic eruptions etc.

2. *Aadhibhautika*: The known factors around us like accidents, human contacts, pollution, crime etc.

3. *Aadhyaatmika*: Problems of our bodies and minds like diseases, anger, frustrations etc.

We sincerely pray to the Lord that at least while we undertake special tasks or even in our daily lives, there are no problems or that, problems are minimised from the three sources written about above. May peace alone prevail. Hence *shaanti* is chanted thrice.

It is chanted aloud the first time, addressing the unseen forces. It is chanted softer the second time, directed to our immediate surroundings and those around, and softest the last time as it is addressed to oneself.

Why do we offer a coconut?

In India one of the most common offerings in a temple is a coconut. It is also offered on occasions like weddings, festivals, the use of a new vehicle, bridge, house etc. A pot (*kalasha*) full of water, adorned with mango leaves and a coconut on top is worshipped on important occasions and used to receive revered guests.

It is offered in the sacrificial fire whilst performing *homa*. The coconut is broken and placed before the Lord. It is later distributed as *prasaada*. It is offered to please the Lord or to fulfill our desires.

There was a time when animal sacrifice (*bali*) was practised, symbolising the offering of our animalistic tendencies to the Lord. Slowly this practice faded and the coconut was offered instead. The fibre covering of the dried coconut is removed except for a tuft on

the top. The marks on the coconut make it look like the head of a human being. The coconut is broken, symbolising the breaking of the ego. The juice within, representing the inner tendencies (*vaasanas*) is offered along with the white kernel – the mind, to the Lord. A mind thus purified by the touch of the Lord is used as *prasaada* (a holy gift).

In the traditional *abhishekha* ritual done in all temples and many homes, several materials are poured over the deity like milk, curd, honey, tender coconut water, sandal paste, holy ash etc. Each material has a specific significance of bestowing certain benefits on worshippers. Tender coconut water is used in *abhisheka* rituals since it is believed to bestow spiritual growth on the seeker.

The coconut also symbolises selfless service. Every part of the tree – the trunk, leaves, fruit, coir etc. is used in innumerable ways like thatches, mats, tasty dishes, oil, soap etc. It takes in even salty water from the earth and converts it into sweet nutritive water that is especially beneficial to sick people. It is used in the preparation of many ayurvedic medicines and in other alternative medicinal systems.

The marks on the coconut are even thought to represent the three-eyed Lord Shiva and therefore it is considered to be a means to fulfill our desires. In certain rituals a coconut is placed on a *kalasha*, decorated, garlanded and worshipped as symbolic of Lord Shiva and of the man of realisation (*gnaani*).

Why do we chant *Om?*

*O*m is one of the most chanted sound symbols in India. It has a profound effect on the body and mind of the one who chants and also on the surroundings. Most *mantras* and *vedic* prayers start with *Om*. All auspicious actions begin with *Om*. It is even used as a greeting – *Om, Hari Om* etc. It is repeated as a *mantra* or meditated upon. Its form is worshipped, contemplated upon or used as an auspicious sign.

❖ Why do we chant *Om?*

Om is the universal name of the Lord. It is made up of the letters A (phonetically as in "around"), U (phonetically as in "put") and M (phonetically as in "mum"). The sound emerging from the vocal chords starts from the base of the throat as "A". With the coming together of the lips, "U" is formed and when the lips are closed, all sound ends in "M". The three

letters symbolise the three states (waking, dream and deep sleep), the three deities (Brahma, Vishnu and Shiva), the three *Vedas* (*Rig, Yajur* and *Sama*) the three worlds (*Bhuh, Bhuvah, Suvah*) etc. The Lord is all these and beyond. The formless, attributeless Lord (*Brahman*) is represented by the silence between two *Om* chants. *Om* is also called *pranava* that means "that (symbol or sound) by which the Lord is praised". The entire essence of the *Vedas* is enshrined in the word *Om*.

It is said that the Lord started creating the world after chanting *Om* and *atha*. Hence its sound is considered to create an auspicious beginning for any task that we undertake.

The *Om* chant should have the resounding sound of a bell (aaooommm). It fills the mind with peace, makes it focussed and replete with subtle sound. People meditate on its meaning and attain realisation.

Om is written in different ways in different places. The most common form (ॐ) symbolises Lord Ganesha. The upper curve is the head; the lower large one, the stomach; the side one, the trunk; and the semi-circular mark with the dot, the sweet-meat ball (*modaka*) in Lord Ganesha's hand.

Thus *Om* symbolises everything – the means and the goal of life, the world and the Truth behind it, the material and the Sacred, all forms and the Formless.

74

Why do we do *aarati?*

Towards the end of every ritualistic worship (*pooja* or *bhajan*) of the Lord or to welcome an honoured guest or saint, we perform the *aarati.* This is always accompanied by the ringing of the bell and sometimes by singing, playing of musical instruments and clapping.

It is one of the sixteen steps (*shodasha upachaara*) of the *pooja* ritual. It is referred to as the auspicious light (*mangala niraajanam*). Holding the lighted lamp in the right hand, we wave the flame in a clockwise circling movement to light the entire form of the Lord. Each part is revealed individually and also the entire form of the Lord. As the light is waved we either do mental or loud chanting of prayers or simply behold the beautiful form of the Lord, illumined by the lamp. We experience an added intensity in our prayers and the Lord's image seems to manifest a special beauty at that time. At the end of the *aarati*

we place our hands over the flame and then gently touch our eyes and the top of the head.

We have seen and participated in this ritual from our childhood. Let us find out why we do the *aarati?*

Having worshipped the Lord with love – performing *abhisheka*, decorating the image and offering fruits and delicacies, we see the beauty of the Lord in all His glory. Our minds are focussed on each limb of the Lord as it is lit up by the lamp. It is akin to silent open-eyed meditation on His beauty. The singing, clapping, ringing of the bell etc. denote the joy and auspiciousness which accompanies the vision of the Lord.

Aarati is often performed with camphor. This holds a telling spiritual significance. Camphor when lit burns itself out completely without leaving a trace of it. Camphor represents our inherent tendencies (*vaasanas*). When lit by the fire of knowledge which illumines the Lord (Truth), our *vaasanas* thereafter burn themselves out completely, not leaving a trace of the ego which creates in us a sense of individuality that keeps us separate from the Lord. Also while camphor burns to reveal the glory of the Lord, it emits a pleasant perfume even while it sacrifices itself. In our spiritual progress, even as we serve the guru and society, we should willingly sacrifice ourselves and all we have, to spread the "perfume" of love to all.

We often wait a long while to see the illumined Lord but when the *aarati* is actually performed, our eyes close automatically as if to look within. This is to signify that each of us is a temple of the Lord – we hold the divinity within. Just as the priest reveals the form of the Lord clearly with the *aarati* flame, so too the guru clearly reveals to us the divinity within each one of us with the help of the "flame" of knowledge (or the light of spiritual knowledge). At the end of the *aarati*, we place our hands over the flame and then touch our eyes and the top of the head. It means – may the light that illumined the Lord light up my vision; may my vision be divine and my thoughts noble and beautiful.

The philosophical meaning of *aarati* extends further. The sun, moon, stars, lightning and fire are the natural sources of light. The Lord is the source of all these wondrous phenomena of the universe. It is due to Him alone that all else exist and shine. As we light up the Lord with the flame of the *aarati*, we turn our attention to the very source of all light which symbolises knowledge and life.

Also the sun is the presiding deity of the intellect; the moon, that of the mind; and fire, that of speech. The Lord is the supreme Consciousness that illumines all of them. Without Him the intellect cannot think, nor can the mind feel nor the tongue speak. The Lord is beyond the mind, intellect and speech. How can these finite equipment illumine the infinite Lord? Therefore as we perform the *aarati* we chant:

न तत्र सूर्यो भाति न चन्द्र तारकम्
  नेमा विद्युतो भान्ति कुतोऽयमग्निः।
तमेव भान्तमनुभाति सर्वम्
  तस्य भासा सर्वमिदं विभाति।।

Na tatra suryo bhaati na chandra taarakam
  Nemaa vidyuto bhaanti kutoyamagnih
Tameva bhaantam anubhaati sarvam
  Tasya bhaasa sarvam idam vibhaati

He is there where the sun does not shine,
  Nor the moon, stars and lightning.
Then what to talk of this small flame
  (in my hand)!
Everything (in the universe) shines
  only after the Lord,
And by His light alone are we all illumined.